Name: _____

CEM

Verbal Reasoning & Cloze Procedure

11+ Practice Papers

Alison Head

GALORE PARK

AN HACHETTE UK COMPANY

CEM (Durham University) produce annual 11+ tests (CEM Select Entrance Assessments) for independent schools and selective state schools and do not make past papers available to pupils. However, the feedback from our specialist team of 11+ tutors, independent schools' teachers, test writers and specialist authors enables us to provide you with a series of tests equipping your child with the highest level preparation. This publication covers a range of questions representative of the CEM assessments, tracking trends and levels of difficulty from recent years, based on our feedback. Tests change from year to year and there is therefore no guarantee that all question types your child will encounter are represented in this publication.

Please note: Hachette UK is not associated with CEM or linked to Durham University in any way. These tests do not include any official questions and they are not endorsed by CEM or Durham University. 'CEM', 'Centre for Evaluation and Monitoring', 'Durham University' and 'The University of Durham' are all trademarks of Durham University.

Orders: **Teachers** please contact Bookpoint Ltd, 130 Park Drive, Milton Park, Abingdon, Oxon OX14 4SE. Telephone: (44) 01235 400555. Email primary@bookpoint.co.uk. Lines are open from 9 a.m. to 5 p.m., Monday to Saturday, with a 24-hour message answering service.

Parents, Tutors please call: 020 3122 6405 (Monday to Friday, 9:30 a.m. to 4.30 p.m.). Email: parentenquiries@galorepark.co.uk

Visit our website at www.galorepark.co.uk for details of other revision guides for Common Entrance, examination papers and Galore Park publications.

ISBN: 978 1 5104 4973 2

© Alison Head 2019
First published in 2019 by
Hodder & Stoughton Limited
An Hachette UK Company
Carmelite House
50 Victoria Embankment
London EC4Y 0DZ
www.galorepark.co.uk
Impression number   10 9 8 7 6 5 4 3 2 1
Year   2023 2022 2021 2020 2019

Typeset in India
Printed in the UK

A catalogue record for this title is available from the British Library.

MIX
Paper from
responsible sources
FSC™ C104740
FSC
www.fsc.org

Contents and progress record

Section	Page	Length (no. Qs)	Timing (mins)	Question type	Score	Time
Paper 1 Foundation level Representing a CEM test at an average level of challenge for grammar and independent schools.						
Synonyms	9	20	7	Multiple choice	/ 20	:
Spot the difference	12	14	5	Multiple choice	/ 14	:
Match the meaning	14	14	6	Multiple choice	/ 14	:
Cloze procedure: choose a word to fit a space	16	20	10	Multiple choice	/ 20	:
				Total	/ 68	:
Paper 2 Standard level Representing a CEM test at a medium level of challenge for grammar and independent schools.						
Cloze procedure: complete the sentence	19	24	12	Mixed	/ 24	:
Antonyms	21	14	5	Mixed	/ 14	:
Spot the difference	24	20	7	Mixed	/ 20	:
Order the sentence	27	12	7	Mixed	/ 12	:
				Total	/ 70	:
Paper 3 Standard / advanced level Representing a CEM test at a medium to high level of challenge for grammar and independent schools.						
Synonyms and antonyms	30	24	12	Mixed	/ 24	:
Cloze procedure: choose a word to fit a space	34	20	10	Mixed	/ 20	:
Order the sentence	37	12	7	Mixed	/ 12	:
Match the meaning	39	14	6	Mixed	/ 14	:
				Total	/ 70	:

Section	Page	Length (no. Qs)	Timing (mins)	Question type	Score	Time
Paper 4 Advanced level Representing a CEM test at a high level of challenge for independent schools.						
Find the missing letters	41	18	8	Standard	/ 18	:
Cloze procedure: complete the sentence	43	20	10	Standard	/ 20	:
Antonyms	45	26	9	Standard	/ 26	:
Cloze procedure: choose a word to fit a space	47	14	8	Standard	/ 14	:
				Total	/ 78	:

Go to the Galore Park website to download the free PDF answer sheets to use and re-use as many times as you need: galorepark.co.uk/answersheets

How to use this book

Introduction

These practice papers have been written to provide final preparation for your CEM 11+ verbal reasoning test. To give you the best chance of success, Galore Park has worked with 11+ tutors, independent schools' teachers, test writers and specialist authors to create these practice papers.

This book includes four model papers. Each paper contains 68–78 multiple-choice and standard questions, testing a variety of skills. The papers increase in difficulty from Paper 1 to Paper 4 and all work to a timing that is typical of CEM tests in the past. This is because CEM tests can change in difficulty both from year to year and from school to school.

So that you experience how the CEM tests work, we have included a few key elements to help you become familiar with what to expect:

- Not all of the question types will appear in each paper and some may occur more than once.
- Each test lasts between 28 and 35 minutes (there are often many questions that you may not complete in the time given).
- The sections (or **parts**) within each paper are short and of unpredictable length.
- Each part begins with an untimed introduction and a training question to explain the question format.

It is important to read the instructions carefully as you will be asked to record your answers in a variety of ways:

- choosing a multiple-choice option using a separate answer sheet
- choosing a multiple-choice option, writing / recording this on the paper itself.

These different styles are included because the online tests expect you to be able to adapt to different question formats quickly as you move on from one part of a paper to the next. These formats can also change from year to year.

As you mark your answers, you will see references to the Galore Park *11+ Verbal Reasoning Study and Revision Guide*. These references have been included so that you can go straight to some useful revision tips and find extra practice questions for those areas where you would like more help.

Working through the book

The **Contents and progress record** on pages 3–4 helps you to track your scores and timings as you work through the papers.

You may find some of the questions hard, but don't worry – these tests are designed to make you think. Agree with your parents on a good time to take the test and follow the instructions below to prepare for each paper as if you are actually going to sit your Pre-test/11+ verbal reasoning test.

1 Read the instructions on page 8 before you begin each practice paper.
2 Download the **answer sheet** from galorepark.co.uk/answersheets and print it out before you begin.
3 Take the test in a quiet room. Set a timer and record your answers as instructed.
4 Note down how long the test takes you (all questions should be completed even if you run over the time suggested). If possible, complete a whole paper in one session.
5 Mark the paper using the answers at the back of the book.
6 Go through the paper again with a friend or parent, talk about the difficult questions and note which parts of the revision guide you are going to review.

The **Answers** can be cut out so that you can mark your papers easily. Do not look at the answers until you have attempted a whole paper.

When you have finished a test, turn back to the **Contents and progress record** and fill in the boxes. Make sure to write your total number of marks and time taken in the **Score** and **Time** boxes.

If you would like to take further CEM-style papers after completing this book, you will find more papers in the *Pre-test/11+ Verbal Reasoning Practice Papers 1* and *2* (see **Continue your learning journey** on page 7).

Test day tips

Take time to prepare yourself on the day before you go for the test. Remember to take sharpened pencils, an eraser and, if you are allowed, water to maintain your concentration levels and a watch to time yourself.

… and don't forget to have breakfast before you go!

Pre-test and the 11+ entrance exams

This title is part of the Galore Park *Pre-test/11+* series and there are three further *Verbal Reasoning Practice Paper* titles (see **Continue your learning journey** on page 7).

This series is designed to help you prepare for pre-tests and 11+ entrance exams if you are applying to independent schools. These exams are often the same as those set by local grammar schools.

Pre-tests and 11+ verbal reasoning tests appear in a variety of formats and lengths and it is likely that if you are applying for more than one school, you will encounter more than one of style of test. These include:

● Pre-test/11+ entrance exams in different formats from GL, CEM and ISEB
● Pre-test/11+ entrance exams created specifically for particular schools.

As the tests change all the time it can be difficult to predict the questions, making them harder to revise for. If you are taking more than one style of test, review the books in the **Continue your learning journey** section to see which other titles could be helpful to you.

For parents

For your child to get the maximum benefit from these papers, they should complete them in conditions as close as possible to those they will face in the actual test, as described in the **Working through the book** section on page 5.

Working with your child to follow up the revision work suggested in the answers can improve their performance in areas where they are less confident and boost their chances of success.

For teachers and tutors

As the papers get progressively more difficult, they offer practice in increasing speed at answering questions required in the most challenging verbal reasoning tests.

The answer sheets provide helpful practice in recording answers on a separate document.

Remediation suggested in the answers, referencing the *Revision Guide*, can be helpful for follow-up revision having completed the paper.

Continue your learning journey

When you have completed these *Practice Papers*, you can carry on your learning right up until exam day with the following resources.

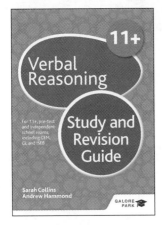   

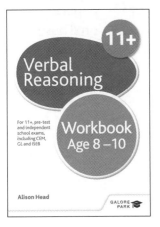 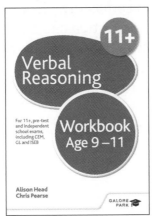 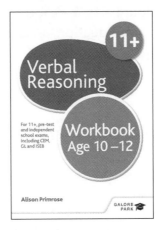

The *Revision Guide* (referenced in the answers to this book) covers basic skills in all areas of verbal reasoning, and guidance is provided on how to improve in this subject.

Pre-test/11+ Practice Papers 1 and *2* are designed to provide a complete revision experience across the various test styles you may encounter. Between the two titles there are eighteen tests of varying lengths, each followed by comprehensive answer explanations.

- *Book 1* begins with four training tests, followed by four short papers and two longer format papers designed to develop your confidence and speed.
- *Book 2* contains a further eight model papers and answers to improve your accuracy, speed and ability to deal with variations in question format under pressure.

GL 11+ Verbal Reasoning Practice Papers contains four practice papers designed for preparation for the GL-style tests. Each paper is split into short tests in verbal reasoning. The tests vary in length and format and are excellent for short bursts of timed practice.

The *Workbooks* will further develop your skills with over 220 questions to practise in each book. To prepare you for the exam, these books include more examples of the question variations you meet in these *Practice Papers* – the more times you practise the questions, the better equipped for the exams you will be.

- Age 8–10: Increase your familiarity with variations in the question types.
- Age 9–11: Experiment with further techniques to improve your accuracy.
- Age 10–12: Develop faster response times through consistent practice.

Preparing for each paper

Read these instructions before you begin each practice paper.

1 Take this test in a quiet room. Have your timer ready.
2 Check at the beginning of **Part 1** if you will be recording your answers on an **answer sheet**. If a sheet is required, download it from galorepark.co.uk/answersheets and print it out before you begin.
3 This test is made up of four Parts, 1–4. You should complete all four parts of this paper.
4 Each part begins with an introduction, an example question and a training question. These pages are untimed and you should read these instructions carefully, then complete the training question before beginning the timed questions.
5 Start the timer *after* completing the introduction to each part and *before* you look at the timed questions.
6 Stop the timer at the end of each part, as instructed.
7 For Parts 1–4:
   a aim for the time given
   b complete all questions
   c note the actual time you have taken at the end of each part.
8 Answer the questions as described in the introduction at the beginning of each part, using a pencil.
9 If you want to change an answer as you work through a part, rub your answer out and rewrite it. You cannot change an answer after you have completed a part.
10 Work as quickly and efficiently as you can. If a question is difficult to answer, come back to it after finishing the other questions in that part.
11 Aim to answer each question before you finish, even if you are not completely sure of the answer.
12 *Do not look at the answers before completing the entire paper.* The instructions in **Working through the book** on page 5 explain how to review your answers.

Always read the instructions on exam papers carefully and make sure you understand exactly what you need to do to answer the questions.

Paper 1

Download and print the answer sheet from galorepark.co.uk/answersheets before you start this paper.

Complete all four parts of this paper to the timings given at the start of each part. Stop the timer after completing each part and start it again after answering the training question.

Part 1: Synonyms

Section time: 7 minutes

How to answer these questions

All your answers to this part should be recorded on the answer sheet you have downloaded.

Look at the example and then complete the training question. **Do not begin timing yourself until you have finished this page.**

> ### Example question
> Find the word that means the same or nearly the same as the bold word. Select one of the options A–E to answer the question.
>
> **distort**
>
> A inform   B exhibit   C debate   D warp   E form
>
> A ⬜   B ⬜   C ⬜   D ▬   E ⬜
>
> Answer: **D** warp   Distort and warp both mean to change the shape or alter the meaning of something.

Now answer the training question, recording your answer choice as shown above. The correct answer is at the bottom of this page.

> ### Training question
> **reveal**
>
> A find   B show   C maintain   D conceal   E solve
>
> A ⬜   B ⬜   C ⬜   D ⬜   E ⬜

Use the downloaded answer sheet to record your answers for the questions that follow. You will see the example and training question have already been recorded.

Check your answers only after completing all of Paper 1. The answers are in a cut-out section at the end of the book. Complete the 'results' boxes at the end of this part when you have added up your score. If you run over the time given, complete the questions and note the time you have taken.

Training question answer: **B** show   Reveal and show both mean to display or bare something.

You now have 7 minutes to complete the following 20 questions.

Find the word that means the same or nearly the same as the bold word. Select one of the options A–E to answer each question.

1 **make** (1)

   A fabric   B brick   C produce   D purchase   E find

2 **simple** (1)

   A small   B lost   C busy   D easy   E fast

3 **huge** (1)

   A whale   B wall   C large   D weigh   E size

4 **hurry** (1)

   A late   B rush   C roll   D time   E wait

5 **talk** (1)

   A noise   B words   C speak   D listen   E ear

6 **bang** (1)

   A break   B storm   C soft   D tap   E crash

7 **jump** (1)

   A play   B leap   C stop   D flat   E stride

8 **neat** (1)

   A best   B nest   C few   D tidy   E dirt

9 **tired** (1)

   A rest   B weary   C awake   D energy   E flow

10 **enemy** (1)

   A fight   B friend   C angry   D foe   E reveal

11 **brag** (1)

   A brown   B argue   C arrange   D escape   E boast

12 **bottle** (1)

   A water   B case   C flask   D lid   E empty

13 **coast** (1)

   A sail   B land   C sure   D float   E shore

14 **origin** (1)

   A stem   B route   C task   D root   E plant

15 beam (1)

A sun   B lamp   C flare   D shade   E golden

16 bear (1)

A strong   B link   C support   D fierce   E spring

17 shaft (1)

A stick   B stem   C path   D tunnel   E road

18 waste (1)

A dust   B lose   C middle   D squander   E discard

19 void (1)

A gape   B sky   C valid   D gap   E solid

20 furnish (1)

A chair   B build   C supply   D arrange   E steal

Now move on to Part 2.
Record your results for *Synonyms* here
after you have completed the rest of Paper 1.

Score [ ] /20   Time [ ] : [ ]

Part 2: Spot the difference

How to answer these questions

All your answers to this part should be recorded on the answer sheet you have downloaded.

Look at the example and then complete the training question. **Do not begin timing yourself until you have finished this page.**

> ### Example question
>
> Three of the words in the list are related to each other in some way. Find the word that is not linked to the others. Select one of the options A–D to answer the question.
>
> **A** shred   **B** grate   **C** grill   **D** grind
>
> A ▭   B ▭   C ▬   D ▭
>
> Answer: **C** grill   All of the other words mean to cut into very small pieces.

Now answer the training question, recording your answer choice as shown above. The correct answer is at the bottom of this page.

> ### Training question
>
> **A** bold   **B** daring   **C** brave   **D** fast
>
> A ▭   B ▭   C ▭   D ▭

Use the downloaded answer sheet to record your answers for the questions that follow. You will see the example and training question have already been recorded.

Check your answers only after completing all of Paper 1. The answers are in a cut-out section at the end of the book. Complete the 'results' boxes at the end of this part when you have added up your score. If you run over the time given, complete the questions and note the time you have taken.

Training question answer: **D** fast   All of the other words mean to be without fear.

You now have 5 minutes to complete the following 14 questions.

Select one of the options A–D to answer the question.

1	A blue	B green	C grey	D small	(1)
2	A quick	B quiet	C speedy	D swift	(1)
3	A square	B circle	C oval	D cube	(1)
4	A silver	B gold	C steal	D tin	(1)
5	A huge	B width	C large	D great	(1)
6	A four	B won	C ten	D two	(1)
7	A tiny	B small	C hour	D minute	(1)
8	A ship	B craft	C vessel	D mast	(1)
9	A line	B row	C din	D racket	(1)
10	A globe	B disc	C orb	D ball	(1)
11	A char	B sear	C steam	D burn	(1)
12	A read	B opening	C study	D pore	(1)
13	A step	B leg	C foot	D stage	(1)
14	A leaf	B ream	C sheet	D folio	(1)

Now move on to Part 3.

Record your results for *Spot the difference* here after you have completed the rest of *Paper 1*.

Score ☐ /14 Time ☐:☐

Part 3: Match the meaning

How to answer these questions

All your answers to this part should be recorded on the answer sheet you have downloaded.

Look at the example and then complete the training question. **Do not begin timing yourself until you have finished this page.**

> ### Example question
>
> Choose one word from the list that has a link with the words in both sets of brackets. Select one of the options A–E to answer the question.
>
> (fair, pale)   (lamp, lantern)
>
> | A warm | B light | C glow | D shade | E soft |
> |--------|---------|--------|---------|--------|
> | A ☐ | B ▬▬ | C ☐ | D ☐ | E ☐ |
>
> Answer: **B light** 'light' is an adjective describing something or somebody as having little colour, e.g. a fair or light complexion; it is also a noun meaning an object that gives light such as a lamp or lantern.
>
> fair, pale, light   lamp, lantern, light

Now answer the training question, recording your answer choice as shown above. The correct answer is at the bottom of this page.

> ### Training question
>
> (brick, piece)   (obstruct, stop)
>
> | A group | B batch | C close | D block | E seal |
> |---------|---------|---------|---------|--------|
> | A ☐ | B ☐ | C ☐ | D ☐ | E ☐ |

Use the downloaded answer sheet to record your answers for the questions that follow. You will see the example and training question have already been recorded.

Check your answers only after completing all of Paper 1. The answers are in a cut-out section at the end of the book. Complete the 'results' boxes at the end of this part when you have added up your score. If you run over the time given, complete the questions and note the time you have taken.

Training question answer: **D block** 'block' is a noun meaning brick or piece of something; it is also a verb meaning to obstruct or stop something.

You now have 6 minutes to complete the following 14 questions.

Select one of the options A–E to answer the question.

1 (soar, glide)   (bee, moth) (1)
  A high   B fly   C sky   D air   E wind

2 (jump, leap)   (summer, winter) (1)
  A wind   B spring   C rain   D hope   E twist

3 (run, rush)   (competition, contest) (1)
  A speed   B lane   C race   D win   E team

4 (lid, stopper)   (hat, bonnet) (1)
  A cap   B stop   C top   D tap   E fold

5 (exercise, prepare)   (plane, car) (1)
  A practice   B drive   C team   D train   E rail

6 (glue, fasten)   (twig, branch) (1)
  A tree   B stick   C gum   D bark   E brown

7 (dish, basin)   (throw, hurl) (1)
  A plate   B bowl   C serve   D fork   E rise

8 (stem, shoot)   (follow, pursue) (1)
  A track   B branch   C path   D stalk   E chase

9 (alter, transform)   (coins, money) (1)
  A prize   B buy   C donate   D change   E gift

10 (carry, bring)   (wagon, trolley) (1)
  A haul   B bag   C cart   D collect   E lug

11 (guide, steer)   (copper, zinc) (1)
  A melt   B lead   C steal   D conduct   E rule

12 (bore, pierce)   (practice, routine) (1)
  A repeat   B tire   C punch   D drill   E brace

13 (outline, shape)   (digit, character) (1)
  A number   B count   C figure   D draw   E measure

14 (word, name)   (session, time) (1)
  A meaning B term   C lesson   D learn   E spell

Now move on to Part 4.
**Record your results for *Match the meaning*
here *after you have completed the rest of
Paper 1*.**

Score		/14	Time		:	

Part 4: Cloze procedure: choose a word to fit a space

How to answer these questions

All your answers to this part should be recorded on the answer sheet you have downloaded.

Look at the example and then complete the training question. **Do not begin timing yourself until you have finished this page.**

Example question

Choose the best word from the list to complete the sentence. Select one of the options A–E to answer the question.

Theme parks are a _____ place for families to visit.

A busy	B popular	C local	D trip	E journey
A ▢	B ▬	C ▢	D ▢	E ▢

Answer: **B** popular   Theme parks are a <u>popular</u> place for families to visit.

Now answer the training question, recording your answer choice as shown above. The correct answer is at the bottom of this page.

Training question

The teacher displayed the children's _____ on the walls.

A coats	B learn	C art	D school	E today
A ▢	B ▢	C ▢	D ▢	E ▢

Use the downloaded answer sheet to record your answers for the questions that follow. You will see the example and training question have already been recorded.

Check your answers only after completing all of Paper 1. The answers are in a cut-out section at the end of the book. Complete the 'results' boxes at the end of this part when you have added up your score. If you run over the time given, complete the questions and note the time you have taken.

You now have 10 minutes to complete the following 20 questions.
Select one of the options A–E to answer the question.

1 We _____ conkers from under the tree.   (1)
   A find   B searched   C went   D collected   E fell

2 We ate popcorn _____ we watched the film.   (1)
   A so   B while   C between   D visit   E cinema

3 Carrot sticks make a _____ snack.   (1)
   A hungry   B orange   C lunch   D healthy   E short

4 They walked too _____ so they missed the train.   (1)
   A fast   B stroll   C station   D slowly   E early

5 I cannot _____ for my party next week.   (1)
   A sleep   B wait   C invite   D celebration   E look

6 The children _____ what they wanted to eat.   (1)
   A lose   B chose   C menu   D wait   E drink

7 The actors in the play were very _____ .   (1)
   A theatre   B lost   C script   D talk   E talented

8 Fragile things are _____ broken.   (1)
   A better   B easily   C special   D new   E shattered

9 Heavy downpours are _____ for this afternoon.   (1)
   A planned   B imagine   C necessary   D forecast   E perhaps

10 Mum carefully planned our _____ to the seaside.   (1)
   A distance   B travelling   C route   D signs   E roads

11 You must look both ways _____ crossing the road.   (1)
   A for   B because   C so   D before   E safety

12 The girls trained hard to _____ for the race.   (1)
   A participate B enter   C win   D ensure   E prepare

13 New homes were built on the _____ of the old car park.   (1)
   A plan   B site   C view   D scheme   E home

14 I was _____ to win a prize in the raffle.   (1)
   A first   B brave   C certainly   D fortune   E lucky

15 Mia loves books with _____ endings. (1)

    A unexpected B final   C stop   D first   E character

16 The museum _____ many artefacts from Ancient Egypt. (1)

    A homes   B shelves   C conserves   D exploits   E manages

17 In medieval times, the _____ for stealing were severe. (1)

    A effects   B penalties   C conviction   D appeal   E offence

18 A clap of thunder shattered the _____ of the forest glade. (1)

    A seclusion   B turbulence   C privacy   D tranquility   E bustle

19 I was _____ by the huge choice on the dessert menu. (1)

    A disturbed   B bewildered   C determined   D decisive   E lost

20 Everyone hastily _____ the building when the alarm sounded. (1)

    A abandoned B alarmed   C evaluated   D approached   E evacuated

Record your results for *Choose a word to fit a space* here.

Score [ ] /20 Time [ ] : [ ]

Record your total score and time for Paper 1 here.

Score [ ] /68 Time [ ] : [ ]

Paper 2

Complete all four parts of this paper to the timings given at the start of each part. Stop the timer after completing each part and start it again after answering the training question.

Part 1: Cloze procedure: complete the sentence

Section time: 12 minutes

How to answer these questions

All your answers to this part should be recorded on this paper.

Complete your answers, as instructed, on the lines provided. Look at the example and then complete the training question. **Do not begin timing yourself until you have finished this page.**

> Example question
>
> Read the sentence below and insert the correct letters to complete the words.
>
> Big Ben is in a very tall __ l __ __ k tower that is often seen on
> p __ __ __ c __ __ __ s of London.
> Answer: Big Ben is in a very tall c l o c k tower that is often seen on p o s t c a r d s of London.

Now answer the training question, writing in your answers as shown above. The correct answer is at the bottom of this page.

> Training question
> Orangutans are __ a __ __ v __ to Borneo and Sumatra and live in the __ a __ n
> f __ r __ __ __ s.

Record your answers for the questions that follow in the spaces provided.

Check your answers only after completing all of Paper 2. The answers are in a cut-out section at the end of the book. Complete the 'results' boxes at the end of this part when you have added up your score. If you run over the time given, complete the questions and note the time you have taken.

Training question answer: native, rainforests   Orangutans are native to Borneo and Sumatra and live in the rainforests.

You now have 12 minutes to complete the following 24 questions.

1   The Sun s __ __ n __ all day yesterday.   (1)

2   Max c __ __ __ __ t a cold last week.   (1)

3 & 4   Our __ c h __ __ l trip to the t h __ __ __ r e was brilliant.   (2)

5   We arrived at the __ t __ t i __ n just as our train came into view.   (1)

6   They ate s __ l __ __ with their pizza.   (1)

7 & 8   Tia b __ r __ o __ e __ two books from the __ i b __ a __ y.   (2)

9   E __ e r __ __ __ e is important as part of a healthy lifestyle.   (1)

10   The thunderstorm last night was very d r __ m __ __ __ c.   (1)

11   The homework task was not d i __ __ i c __ l t.   (1)

12   Our __ a __ s p __ __ t s were checked at the airport.   (1)

13   My cousins e__ __ g r __ t __ d to Spain.   (1)

14   Mum cooked our burgers on the __ a __ __ e c __ __.   (1)

15 & 16 Windsor C __ s __ l e was badly __ a __ a g __ __ by fire in 1992.   (2)

17   Our school football team won the __ e a __ __ __ last year.   (1)

18   Swimming in the sea can be __ a __ __ __ r __ __ s.   (1)

19 & 20 Many __ i l l __ __ e s in England have interesting t __ a d __ t __ __ n s.   (2)

21 & 22 The a l __ __ c __ is an animal that __ r __ g __ n a __ __ d in
         South America.   (2)

23   The c a __ p __ __ t e we stayed at was well equipped.   (1)

24   I need to get some __ t a __ __ o __ __ r y for the new term.   (1)

Now move on to Part 2.
Record your results for *Complete the*
sentence* here *after you have completed
the rest of Paper 2.

Score [   ] /24   Time [   ]:[   ]

20

Part 2: Antonyms

How to answer these questions

All your answers to this part should be recorded on this paper.

Complete your answers as instructed below. Look at the example and then complete the training question. **Do not begin timing yourself until you have finished this page.**

> ### Example question
>
> Find the word that means the opposite or nearly the opposite of the bold word. Select one of the options A–E to answer the question, then circle the letter below the correct answer.
>
> **praise**
>
> | reward | preach | raise | criticise | practise |
> |--------|--------|-------|-----------|----------|
> | A | B | C | (D) | E |
>
> Answer: **D** criticise   'praise' means to tell somebody how well they have done; 'criticise' means to pick fault.

Now answer the training question, recording your answer as shown above. The correct answer is at the bottom of this page.

> ### Training question
> **reveal**
>
> | discover | lose | conceal | destroy | deter |
> |----------|------|---------|---------|-------|
> | A | B | C | D | E |

Record your answers for the questions that follow on this paper.

Check your answers only after completing all of Paper 2. The answers are in a cut-out section at the end of the book. Complete the 'results' boxes at the end of this part when you have added up your score. If you run over the time given, complete the questions and note the time you have taken.

Training question answer: C conceal   'reveal' means to make something public; 'conceal' means to hide something.

You now have 5 minutes to complete the following 14 questions.

Circle the letter beneath each correct answer.

1 **appear** (1)

view	vanish	see	react	allow
A	B	C	D	E

2 **huge** (1)

great	mean	vast	tiny	grow
A	B	C	D	E

3 **slow** (1)

creep	still	steady	rapid	real
A	B	C	D	E

4 **throw** (1)

ball	bowl	grab	catch	miss
A	B	C	D	E

5 **wide** (1)

thick	long	narrow	line	small
A	B	C	D	E

6 **assemble** (1)

build	collect	part	dismantle	piece
A	B	C	D	E

7 **accelerate** (1)

speed	rush	break	brake	risk
A	B	C	D	E

8 **safety** (1)

haven	injured	danger	protect	sore
A	B	C	D	E

9 **divide** (1)

sum	unite	separate	whole	comply
A	B	C	D	E

10 **accept** (1)

agree	decide	lie	decline	deny
A	B	C	D	E

11 **accuse** (1)

blame	free	absolve	convict	judge
A	B	C	D	E

12 recollect (1)

review	ignore	banish	forget	restore
A	B	C	D	E

13 submit (1)

overhaul	flee	resist	provide	argue
A	B	C	D	E

14 condense (1)

large	shrink	gas	evaporate	water
A	B	C	D	E

Now move on to Part 3.
Record your results for *Antonyms* here
after you have completed the rest of Paper 2.

Score ☐ /14 Time ☐ : ☐

Part 3: Spot the difference

How to answer these questions

All your answers to this part should be recorded on this paper.

Look at the example and then complete the training question. **Do not begin timing yourself until you have finished this page.**

Example question

Three of the words in the list are related to each other in some way. Find the word that is **not** linked to the others. Circle the letter beneath the correct answer choice.

shred   grate   grill   grind

A   B   Ⓒ   D

Answer: **C** grill   All of the other words mean to cut into very small pieces.

Now answer the training question, recording your answer choice as shown above. The correct answer is at the bottom of this page.

Training question

protect   guard   expose   defend

A   B   C   D

Record your answers for the questions that follow on this paper.

Check your answers only after completing all of Paper 2. The answers are in a cut-out section at the end of the book. Complete the 'results' boxes at the end of this part when you have added up your score. If you run over the time given, complete the questions and note the time you have taken.

Training question answer: C expose   All of the other words mean to keep something safe.

You now have 7 minutes to complete the following 20 questions.

Circle the letter beneath each correct answer.

1   thumb   palm   toe   finger   (1)
    A   B   C   D

2   France   Spain   Africa   Holland   (1)
    A   B   C   D

3   cherry   orange   apple   pea   (1)
    A   B   C   D

4   maple   acorn   oak   birch   (1)
    A   B   C   D

5   wind   snow   winter   hail   (1)
    A   B   C   D

6   cut   join   chop   slice   (1)
    A   B   C   D

7   chair   stool   seat   chest   (1)
    A   B   C   D

8   bolt   screw   spanner   nail   (1)
    A   B   C   D

9   technique   approach   action   strategy   (1)
    A   B   C   D

10 road   route   street   lane   (1)
    A   B   C   D

11 disperse   reduce   lessen   contract   (1)
    A   B   C   D

12 compact   small   solid   hard   (1)
    A   B   C   D

13 trap   stall   capture   catch   (1)
    A   B   C   D

14 insult   annoy   anger   fury   (1)
    A   B   C   D

15	store	pack	horde	crowd	(1)
	A	B	C	D	
16	warrant	permit	merit	deserve	(1)
	A	B	C	D	
17	understand	fulfil	achieve	realise	(1)
	A	B	C	D	
18	settle	occupy	populate	living	(1)
	A	B	C	D	
19	assent	allow	concur	approve	(1)
	A	B	C	D	
20	rate	charge	speed	tempo	(1)
	A	B	C	D	

Now move on to Part 4.

Record your results for *Spot the difference* here *after you have completed the rest of Paper 2*.

Score [ ] /20   Time [ ] : [ ]

Part 4: Order the sentence

How to answer these questions

All your answers to this part should be recorded on this paper.

Look at the example and then complete the training question. **Do not begin timing yourself until you have finished this page.**

Example question

In these muddled sentences there is an extra word. Make the longest sentence possible to identify the extra word. Draw a circle around the letter beneath the correct answer choice.

The extensive country was rain caused the flooding in torrential.

extensive	the	rain	flooding	was
A	B	C	D	(E)

Answer: **E** was   The torrential rain caused extensive flooding in the country.

Now answer the training question, recording your answer choice as shown above. The correct answer is at the bottom of this page.

Training question

It was an went pitch outside when dark we.

pitch	outside	we	an	was
A	B	C	D	E

Record your answers for the questions that follow on this paper.

Check your answers only after completing all of Paper 2. The answers are in a cut-out section at the end of the book. Complete the 'results' boxes at the end of this part when you have added up your score. If you run over the time given, complete the questions and note the time you have taken.

Training question answer: D an   It was pitch dark when we went outside.

You now have 7 minutes to complete the following 12 questions.

Circle the letter beneath each correct answer.

1 We are a whether trip to planning Cardiff. (1)

are	whether	planning	trip	to
A	B	C	D	E

2 You tidy to some need messy your bedroom. (1)

tidy	some	need	messy	bedroom
A	B	C	D	E

3 I shoots growing love from plants seed. (1)

growing	love	plants	shoots	seed
A	B	C	D	E

4 My will meeting friends are me the at cinema. (1)

will	meeting	friends	me	cinema
A	B	C	D	E

5 It is post them getting letters exciting in the. (1)

post	letters	getting	them	exciting
A	B	C	D	E

6 My rather well can be cousins conceited. (1)

rather	well	can	cousins	conceited
A	B	C	D	E

7 I was the match the by time tired the ended. (1)

was	the	tired	time	match
A	B	C	D	E

8 We shells the from home beach collected to us take. (1)

shells	the	collected	us	take
A	B	C	D	E

9 Their community will of all benefit be the donation children in the. (1)

will	community	benefit	the	be
A	B	C	D	E

10 The question to the answer obvious was being when I about thought it. (1)

question	being	answer	obvious	about
A	B	C	D	E

11 I wrong took this mistakenly turning the the station by. (1)

this	wrong	mistakenly	turning	by
A	B	C	D	E

12 The home followed dog its two owners loyal wherever went they. (1)

home	its	they	loyal	went
A	B	C	D	E

Record your results for *Order the sentence* here.

Score ☐ /12 Time ☐:☐

Record your total score and time for Paper 2 here.

Score ☐ /70 Time ☐:☐

Paper 3

Download and print the answer sheet from galorepark.co.uk/answersheets before you start this paper.

Complete all four parts of this paper to the timings given at the start of each part. Stop the timer after completing each part and start it again after answering the training questions.

Part 1: Synonyms and antonyms

Section time: 12 minutes

How to answer these questions

All your answers to this part should be recorded on the answer sheet you have downloaded.

Look at the examples and then complete the training questions. **Do not begin timing yourself until you have finished these pages.**

Example questions

Use the words in the table below to answer the following questions.

A return	B joyful	C plunder	D uneven	E mislaid
F hull	G vanished	H level	I take	J frosted
K curved	L flat	M give	N glad	O metal

1 Find two words that are antonyms for the word 'sorry'.

A ☐   B ▬   C ☐   D ☐   E ☐
F ☐   G ☐   H ☐   I ☐   J ☐
K ☐   L ☐   M ☐   N ▬   O ☐

2 Find two words that are synonyms for the word 'lost'.

A ☐   B ☐   C ☐   D ☐   E ▬
F ☐   G ▬   H ☐   I ☐   J ☐
K ☐   L ☐   M ☐   N ☐   O ☐

Answers:

1 **B, N** joyful, glad   'joyful' and 'glad' both have a nearly opposite meaning to 'sorry', expressing happiness rather than regret.

2 **E, G** mislaid, vanished   'mislaid' and 'vanished' both have a similar meaning to 'lost'.

Now answer the training questions, recording your answer as shown above. The correct answers are at the bottom of this page.

Training questions

Use the words in the table to answer the following questions.

1 Find two words that are antonyms for the word 'straight'.

A ☐ B ☐ C ☐ D ☐ E ☐
F ☐ G ☐ H ☐ I ☐ J ☐
K ☐ L ☐ M ☐ N ☐ O ☐

2 Find two words that are synonyms for the word 'steal'.

A ☐ B ☐ C ☐ D ☐ E ☐
F ☐ G ☐ H ☐ I ☐ J ☐
K ☐ L ☐ M ☐ N ☐ O ☐

Use the downloaded answer sheet to record your answers for the questions that follow. You will see the examples and training questions have already been recorded.

Check your answers only after completing all of Paper 3. The answers are in a cut-out section at the end of the book. Complete the 'results' boxes at the end of this part when you have added up your score. If you run over the time given, complete the questions and note the time you have taken.

You now have 12 minutes to complete the following 24 questions.

A select	B entire	B final	D finest	E dirty
F piece	G filthy	H late	I complete	J wreck
K create	L top	M pick	N devise	O last

1 Find two words that are synonyms for the word 'choose'. (1)
2 Find two words that are antonyms for the word 'clean'. (1)
3 Find two words that are synonyms for the word 'whole'. (1)
4 Find two words that are antonyms for the word 'first'. (1)
5 Find two words that are synonyms for the word 'invent'. (1)
6 Find two words that are antonyms for the word 'worst'. (1)

A sudden	B slumber	C tardy	D damp	E quake
F dull	G tremble	H nap	I blunt	J pop
K late	L drip	M unexpected	N dawdle	O moist

7 Find two synonyms for the word 'sleep'. (1)
8 Find two antonyms for the word 'early'. (1)
9 Find two synonyms for the word 'abrupt'. (1)
10 Find two antonyms for the word 'sharp'. (1)
11 Find two synonyms for the word 'shake'. (1)
12 Find two antonyms for the word 'dry'. (1)

A squat	B track	C bygone	D flawed	E low
F tale	G wile	H bestow	I fling	J story
K present	L past	M chore	N tail	O cunning

13 Find two synonyms for the word 'give'. (1)
14 Find two antonyms for the word 'high'. (1)
15 Find two synonyms for the word 'follow'. (1)
16 Find two antonyms for the word 'present'. (1)
17 Find two synonyms for the word 'narrative'. (1)
18 Find two antonyms for the word 'sincerity'. (1)

A flimsy	B circumspect	C abandon	D glee	E slight
F delight	G winnings	H property	I measured	J steady
K predict	L accurate	M foretell	N reject	O haul

19 Find two synonyms for the word 'triumph'. (1)
20 Find two antonyms for the word 'embrace'. (1)
21 Find two synonyms for the word 'jackpot'. (1)
22 Find two antonyms for the word 'sturdy'. (1)
23 Find two synonyms for the word 'divine'. (1)
24 Find two antonyms for the word 'rash'. (1)

Now move on to Part 2.

Record your results for *Synonyms and antonyms* here *after you have completed the rest of Paper 3*.

Score ☐ /24 Time ☐ : ☐

Part 2: Cloze procedure: choose a word to fit a space

How to answer these questions

All your answers to this part should be recorded on the answer sheet you have downloaded.

Look at the example and then complete the training question. **Do not begin timing yourself until you have finished this page.**

Example question

Choose the best word from the list to complete the sentence. Select one of the options A–E to answer the question.

Theme parks are a _____ place for families to visit.

A busy	**B** popular	**C** local	**D** trip	**E** journey
A ▭	B ▬	C ▭	D ▭	E ▭

Answer: **B** popular   Theme parks are a <u>popular</u> place for families to visit.

Now answer the training question, recording your answer choice as shown above. The correct answer is at the bottom of this page.

Training question

The badly damaged car was _____ away to be repaired.

A driven	**B** stolen	**C** broken	**D** towed	**E** trailed
A ▭	B ▭	C ▭	D ▭	E ▭

Use the downloaded answer sheet to record your answers for the questions that follow. You will see the example and training question have already been recorded.

Check your answers only after completing all of Paper 3. The answers are in a cut-out section at the end of the book. Complete the 'results' boxes at the end of this part when you have added up your score. If you run over the time given, complete the questions and note the time you have taken.

Training question answer: **D** towed   The badly damaged card was <u>towed</u> away to be repaired.

34

You now have 10 minutes to complete the following 20 questions.

Select one of the options A–E to answer the question.

1   The lifeboat _____ the crew of the boat.   (1)

A leaving   B bring   C rescued   D sea   E coast

2   We all laughed _____ the joke was funny.   (1)

A if   B because   was   D will   E amuse

3   It took a _____ time to find a parking space.   (1)

A search   B all   C late   D drive   E long

4   The class _____ up in the playground.   (1)

A lined   B run   C teach   D learn   E draw

5   I am _____ up for a new bike.   (1)

A riding   B pay   C saving   D collecting   E money

6   Alice loves to go bowling _____ her friends.   (1)

A so   B at   C by   D alley   E with

7   In the summer, airports become extremely _____ .   (1)

A travelled   B occupied   C crowded   D hot   E airline

8   Our view of the sea was _____ by trees.   (1)

A growing   B shadowed   C obtained   D obscured   E observed

9   The squirrel dangled _____ from the branch.   (1)

A plainly   B squarely   C precariously   D clawing   E high

10 We made our way _____ over the fragile ice.   (1)

A carelessly   B warily   C danger   D frozen   E mildly

11 Ben was _____ by the end of the race.   (1)

A warm   B winner   C exhausted   D bold   E ran

12 Our cat _____ its claws on the post.   (1)

A stretched   B sharpened   C sliced   D nibbled   E damaged

13 The fragile vase was _____ packaged for the journey.   (1)

A carefully   B finally   C broken   D bought   E fine

14 Volcanoes often form where _____ on the Earth's surface meet.   (1)

A pieces   B magma   C plates   D countries   E oceans

15 In 1666, the Great Fire of London _____ the capital of England. (1)

    A concerned   B devastated   C skirted   D relocated   E battered

16 There are _____ twenty-eight days in the month of February. (1)

    A inevitably   B seldom   C sporadically   D usually   E only

17 Loss of _____ is one of the main reasons a species becomes extinct. (1)

    A prey   B oxygen   C conversation   D habitat   E concern

18 With all jurors in agreement, the verdict was _____ . (1)

    A chosen   B contested   C unanimous   D unfortunate   E damning

19 For animals living in desert regions, sources of food can be _____ . (1)

    A invisible   B scarce   C provided   D absent   E rivalled

20 _____ weather dogged the hikers. (1)

    A Spirited   B Spurning   C Inclement   D Hazy   E Stunted

Now move on to Part 3.
Record your results for *Choose a word to fit a space* here *after you have completed the rest of Paper 3*.

Score [ ] /20   Time [ ] : [ ]

Part 3: Order the sentence

Section time: 7 minutes

How to answer these questions

All your answers to this part should be recorded on the answer sheet you have downloaded.

Look at the example and then complete the training question. **Do not begin timing yourself until you have finished this page.**

> ### Example question
> In these muddled sentences there is an extra word. Make the longest sentence possible to identify the extra word. Select one of the options A–E to answer the question.
>
> The extensive country was rain caused the flooding in torrential.
>
> | A extensive | B the | C rain | D flooding | E was |
> |---|---|---|---|---|
> | A ⬜ | B ⬜ | C ⬜ | D ⬜ | E ▬▬ |
>
> Answer: E was   The torrential rain caused extensive flooding in the country.

Now answer the training question, recording your answer choice as shown above. The correct answer is at the bottom of this page.

> ### Training question
> We because ate its quickly we hungry were.
>
> | A because | B ate | C its | D quickly | E were |
> |---|---|---|---|---|
> | A ⬜ | B ⬜ | C ⬜ | D ⬜ | E ⬜ |

Use the downloaded answer sheet to record your answers for the questions that follow. You will see the example and training question have already been recorded.

Check your answers only after completing all of Paper 3. The answers are in a cut-out section at the end of the book. Complete the 'results' boxes at the end of this part when you have added up your score. If you run over the time given, complete the questions and note the time you have taken.

You now have 7 minutes to complete the following 12 questions.

Select one of the options A–E to answer the question.

1   There some puppies were litter seven in the.   (1)
    A some   B puppies   C were   D litter   E the

2   I got a coat took in case them cold it.   (1)
    A got   B coat   C case   D them   E cold

3   Our assembly will class had a special today.   (1)
    A will   B assembly   C had   D class   E today

4   We summer to going France this are was.   (1)
    A going   B to   C summer   D are   E was

5   The Sun such eased and the burst rain through.   (1)
    A eased   B such   C the   D and   E rain

6   I a bought a postcard it send to to friend.   (1)
    A a   B bought   C it   D to   E send

7   The all paths through forest the looked the all same.   (1)
    A the   B all   C through   D paths   E same

8   It will too be to wet if play it to rain continues to.   (1)
    A it   B will   C to   D if   E play

9   Following took map, left on the we third the turning on the.   (1)
    A we   B on   C the   D left   E took

10 The snow icy, fell covering blanket the garden flake in an.   (1)
    A icy   B fell   C blanket   D flake   E garden

11 Realising more late were, we faster we walked.   (1)
    A late   B more   C were   D we   E faster

12 I bed went to my, early too I excited although to sleep was.   (1)
    A to   B my   C too   D was   E early

Now move on to Part 4.

Record your results for *Order the sentence* here *after you have completed the rest of Paper 3*.

Score [   ] /12   Time [   ] : [   ]

Part 4: Match the meaning

How to answer these questions

All your answers to this part should be recorded on the answer sheet you have downloaded.

Look at the example and then complete the training question. **Do not begin timing yourself until you have finished this page.**

> **Example question**
>
> Choose one word from the list that has a link with the words in both sets of brackets. Select one of the options A–E to answer the question.
>
> (fair, pale)   (lamp, lantern)
>
> **A** warm   **B** light   **C** glow   **D** shade   **E** soft
>
> A ▭   B ▬   C ▭   D ▭   E ▭
>
> Answer: **B light**   Light is an adjective describing something or somebody as having little colour, e.g. a fair or light complexion; it is also a noun meaning an object that gives light, such as a lamp or lantern.
>
> fair, pale, light   lamp, lantern, light

Now answer the training question, recording your answer choice as shown above. The correct answer is at the bottom of this page.

> **Training question**
>
> (line, queue)   (quarrel, dispute)
>
> **A** set   **B** rail   **C** row   **D** scrap   **E** rule
>
> A ▭   B ▭   C ▭   D ▭   E ▭

Use the downloaded answer sheet to record your answers for the questions that follow. You will see the example and training question have already been recorded.

Check your answers only after completing all of Paper 3. The answers are in a cut-out section at the end of the book. Complete the 'results' boxes at the end of this part when you have added up your score. If you run over the time given, complete the questions and note the time you have taken.

Training question answer: **C row**   Row is a noun meaning a procession/line, for example a procession/line of people; it is also a verb meaning to argue about something. Note that the word 'row' is pronounced differently depending on the meaning.

You now have 6 minutes to complete the following 14 questions.

Select one of the options A–E to answer the question.

1 (sway, swing)   (boulder, pebble)   (1)
  A music   B dance   C stone   D rock   E slide

2 (universe, galaxy)   (room, gap)   (1)
  A travel   B space   C star   D blank   E dark

3 (pink, blush)   (lily, tulip)   (1)
  A cheek   B posy   C rose   D petal   E plant

4 (fib, invent)   (rest, recline)   (1)
  A tale   B lie   C dream   D tell   E night

5 (grounds, estate)   (leave, stop)   (1)
  A end   B land   C slow   D park   E wall

6 (strip, belt)   (gang, group)   (1)
  A band   B string   C waist   D crowd   E swell

7 (filter, sieve)   (pressure, stress)   (1)
  A twist   B strain   C wrench   D sort   E stretch

8 (well, fit)   (penalty, charge)   (1)
  A challenge   B race   C form   D fine   E true

9 (hail, signal)   (banner, standard)   (1)
  A sign   B flag   C note   D call   E blow

10 (court, flatter)   (buff, beige)   (1)
  A natural   B plead   C dear   D fawn   E calm

11 (wash, trail)   (stir, rouse)   (1)
  A whip   B rinse   C wake   D tide   E wave

12 (generous, large)   (tolerant, enlightened)   (1)
  A fair   B liberal   C free   D bright   E bold

13 (clasp, catch)   (warp, bow)   (1)
  A buckle   B strap   C collapse   D grasp   E gnarl

14 (intensify, strengthen)   (focus, muse)   (1)
  A reinforce   B study   C emphasise   D scrutinise   E concentrate

Record your results for *Match the meaning* here.

Score [ ] /14   Time [ ] : [ ]

Record your total score and time for Paper 3 here.

Score [ ] /70   Time [ ] : [ ]

Paper 4

Complete all four parts of this paper to the timings given at the start of each part. Stop the timer after completing each part and start it again after answering the training question.

Part 1: Find the missing letters

How to answer these questions

All your answers to this part should be recorded on this paper. Complete your answers, as instructed, on the lines provided.

Look at the example and then complete the training question. **Do not begin timing yourself until you have finished this page.**

> ### Example question
> Complete the words by finding the three missing letters. Insert the correct letters to complete the words.
>
> cam __ __ __ laged   ele __ __ __ nts
> Answer: cam <u>o</u> <u>u</u> <u>f</u> laged   ele <u>p</u> <u>h</u> <u>a</u> nts

Now answer the training question, writing in your answers as shown above. The correct answer is at the bottom of this page.

> ### Training question
> enco __ __ __ ge   abs __ __ __ te

Record your answers for the questions that follow on the lines provided.

Check your answers only after completing all of Paper 4. The answers are in a cut-out section at the end of the book. Complete the 'results' boxes at the end of this part when you have added up your score. If you run over the time given, complete the questions and note the time you have taken.

You now have 8 minutes to complete the following 18 questions.

Insert the correct letters to complete the words.

1	flav __ __ __ ed	ple __ __ __ nt	(1)
2	dis __ __ __ b	vi __ __ __ n	(1)
3	v __ __ __ ical	tro __ __ __ e	(1)
4	ph __ __ __ cal	pin __ __ __ ple	(1)
5	a __ __ __ mn	flo __ __ __ sh	(1)
6	or __ __ __ tal	l __ __ __ gne	(1)
7	pl __ __ __ ic	cla __ __ __ c	(1)
8	com __ __ __ ity	cur __ __ __ n	(1)
9	env __ __ __ pe	pu __ __ __ se	(1)
10	le __ __ __ nt	spa __ __ __ w	(1)
11	ci __ __ __ it	r __ __ __ nge	(1)
12	fli __ __ __ r	cel __ __ __ ity	(1)
13	du __ __ __ on	war __ __ __ r	(1)
14	bis __ __ __ t	et __ __ __ al	(1)
15	pi __ __ __ cle	fo __ __ __ ne	(1)
16	r __ __ __ rse	ph __ __ __ om	(1)
17	la __ __ __ l	l __ __ __ il	(1)
18	re __ __ __ nse	or __ __ __ d	(1)

Now move on to Part 2.

Record your results for *Find the missing letters* here *after you have completed the rest of Paper 4*.

Score ☐ /18 Time ☐ : ☐

Part 2: Cloze procedure: complete the sentence

How to answer these questions

All your answers to this part should be recorded on this paper. Complete your answers, as instructed, on the lines provided.

Look at the example and then complete the training question. **Do not begin timing yourself until you have finished this page.**

Example question

In the sentence below a word has three letters missing; these three letters form a word. Write the three-letter word on the lines provided.

At the football match, the referee blew the w ___ ___ ___ tle for half-time.

Answer: **his**   At the football match, the referee blew the w _h_ _i_ _s_ tle for half-time.

Now answer the training question, writing in your answer as shown above. The correct answer is at the bottom of this page.

Training question
The clap of thunder gave me a f ___ ___ ___ ht.

Record your answers for the questions that follow on the lines provided.

Check your answers only after completing all of Paper 4. The answers are in a cut-out section at the end of the book. Complete the 'results' boxes at the end of this part when you have added up your score. If you run over the time given, complete the questions and note the time you have taken.

Training question answer: **rig**   The clap of thunder gave me a fright.

You now have 10 minutes to complete the following 20 questions.

Insert the correct three-letter words to complete the words.

1 The f __ __ __ ory manufactures cars. (1)

2 We could hear the vo __ __ __ s of the children next door. (1)

3 A s __ __ __ p path led up the hill. (1)

4 I love ba __ __ __ g in our new kitchen. (1)

5 I hunted in the dr __ __ __ r for the missing sock. (1)

6 Bella de __ __ __ ded the goal brilliantly. (1)

7 Sailing is his pass __ __ __ . (1)

8 He looked s __ __ __ t in his new clothes. (1)

9 I am f __ __ __ ing much better today. (1)

10 The diamond ring sp __ __ __ led in the sunlight. (1)

11 Jade f __ __ __ ed her exam. (1)

12 We took the pony back to the s __ __ __ le. (1)

13 It is important to be h __ __ __ st. (1)

14 We sat on the t __ __ __ ace. (1)

15 The ugly building was a real e __ __ __ ore. (1)

16 Sam ad __ __ __ s chocolate cake. (1)

17 The stream me __ __ __ ers through the valley. (1)

18 The grass was p __ __ __ hed by the heat. (1)

19 W __ __ __ s flew everywhere. (1)

20 My family has just bought a new ho __ __ __ . (1)

Now move on to Part 3.

Record your results for *Complete the sentence* here *after you have completed the rest of Paper 4*.

Score [   ] /20 Time [   ] : [   ]

Part 3: Antonyms

How to answer these questions

All your answers to this part should be recorded on this paper. Complete your answers, as instructed, on the lines provided.

Look at the example and then complete the training question. **Do not begin timing yourself until you have finished this page.**

Example question
Insert letters in the gaps to complete the word on the right so it is an antonym or nearly an antonym of the word on the left. Write the missing letters in the spaces provided.

available   t a ___ ___ n
Answer: t a _k_ _e_ n   An antonym for available is taken. The 'ke' completes the word correctly.

Now answer the training question, writing in your answer as shown above. The correct answer is at the bottom of this page.

Training question
flee   pu ___ ___ ue

Record your answers for the questions that follow on the lines provided.

Check your answers only after completing all of Paper 4. The answers are in a cut-out section at the end of the book. Complete the 'results' boxes at the end of this part when you have added up your score. If you run over the time given, complete the questions and note the time you have taken.

Training question answer: **pursue**   An antonym for flee is pursue. The 'rs' completes the word correctly.

45

You now have 9 minutes to complete the following 26 questions.

1	timid	b __ __ ve	(1)
2	above	be __ __ __ th	(1)
3	rigid	f __ __ __ __ ble	(1)
4	generous	st __ __ __ y	(1)
5	sturdy	fr __ __ l	(1)
6	obscure	fa __ __ __ s	(1)
7	cramped	sp __ __ __ __ us	(1)
8	systematic	ra __ __ __ m	(1)
9	benign	h __ __ __ __ le	(1)
10	entire	p __ __ __ __ al	(1)
11	permit	f __ __ __ __ d	(1)
12	perfect	f __ __ __ __ d	(1)
13	assist	h __ __ __ __ r	(1)
14	wisdom	f __ __ __ y	(1)
15	vice	vi __ __ __ e	(1)
16	route	de __ __ __ r	(1)
17	extravagant	f __ __ __ __ l	(1)
18	expedite	d __ __ __ y	(1)
19	modest	fla __ __ o __ __ nt	(1)
20	negate	af __ __ r __	(1)
21	professional	a __ __ t __ __ r	(1)
22	keen	a __ __ t __ __ __ ic	(1)
23	harmony	d __ s __ __ __ d	(1)
24	authentic	r __ __ __ __ c __	(1)
25	facilitate	f __ __ __ st __ ll	(1)
26	endorse	den __ __ __ __ e	(1)

Now move on to Part 4.

Record your results for *Antonyms* here
after you have completed the rest of Paper 4.

Score [ ] /26   Time [ ] : [ ]

Part 4: Cloze procedure: choose a word to fit a space

How to answer these questions

All your answers to this part should be recorded on this paper. Complete your answers by circling the word you choose.

Look at the example and then complete the training question. **Do not begin timing yourself until you have finished this page.**

Example question

Choose one of the words in the brackets to complete the sentence in the most sensible way. Circle the word you choose.

It was getting (nightfall (dark) tired sleepy long) when the family got home.

Answer: **dark** It was getting dark when the family got home.

Now answer the training question, circling your answer as shown above. The correct answer is at the bottom of this page.

Training question

I received an (option date place invitation friend) to the party.

Record your answers for the questions that follow on this paper.

Check your answers only after completing all of Paper 4. The answers are in a cut-out section at the end of the book. Complete the 'results' boxes at the end of this part when you have added up your score. If you run over the time given, complete the questions and note the time you have taken.

You now have 8 minutes to complete the following 14 questions.

1 Some beautiful flowers were (carry   found   delivered   send   grew)
   to the house.   (1)

2 Our (learn   new   past   children   book) teacher has lots of good
   ideas.   (1)

3 Owls catch their (hunting   feathers   prey   nests   quickly) in their
   sharp talons.   (1)

4 A carefully planned diet includes lots of (hungry   nutritious   vitamins
   much   cooked) food.   (1)

5 Our hotel had an (rewarding   important   scene   image
   impressive) view of the sea.   (1)

6 Sally (confessed   confided   regretted   accused   whispered)
   in me and made me promise to keep her secret.   (1)

7 It is (essential   earlier   deadline   learning   rightly) that all
   homework is completed.   (1)

8 The (awaited   watching   inhabit   centenary   settle) celebrations
   marked the town's one hundredth anniversary.   (1)

9 I could not see clearly through the (clear   shatter   opaque
   watching   glazier) glass.   (1)

10 Rich Victorian factory owners often (labouring   exploited   peril
   machinery   paid) children, making them do dangerous work for very
   little money.   (1)

11 The equator separates the northern and southern (poles   hemispheres
   section   global   oceans).   (1)

12 Legendary outlaw Robin Hood (sought   veiled   rode   evaded
   bestowed) capture, robbing the rich to give to the poor.   (1)

13 Native to China, panda bears feed (consequently   exclusively   absolute
   currently   some) on bamboo.   (1)

14 Reducing plastic waste has become an (emergency   environmental
   emerge   natural   public) priority.   (1)

Record your results for *Choose a word to fit a space* here.

Score [   ] /14   Time [   ]:[   ]

Record your total score and time for Paper 4 here.

Score [   ] /78   Time [   ]:[   ]

Answers

All the references in the boxes below refer to the *11+ Verbal Reasoning Study and Revision Guide* (ISBN: 9781471849244) so you know exactly where to find out more about the question and your answer.

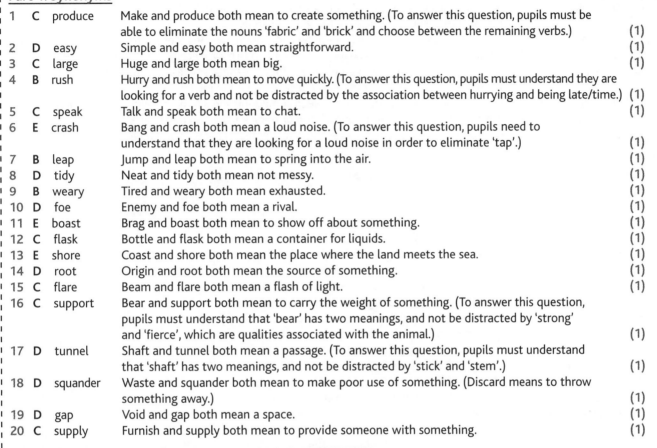

PAPER 1

Part 1: Synonyms

1	C	produce	Make and produce both mean to create something. (To answer this question, pupils must be able to eliminate the nouns 'fabric' and 'brick' and choose between the remaining verbs.)	(1)
2	D	easy	Simple and easy both mean straightforward.	(1)
3	C	large	Huge and large both mean big.	(1)
4	B	rush	Hurry and rush both mean to move quickly. (To answer this question, pupils must understand they are looking for a verb and not be distracted by the association between hurrying and being late/time.)	(1)
5	C	speak	Talk and speak both mean to chat.	(1)
6	E	crash	Bang and crash both mean a loud noise. (To answer this question, pupils need to understand that they are looking for a loud noise in order to eliminate 'tap'.)	(1)
7	B	leap	Jump and leap both mean to spring into the air.	(1)
8	D	tidy	Neat and tidy both mean not messy.	(1)
9	B	weary	Tired and weary both mean exhausted.	(1)
10	D	foe	Enemy and foe both mean a rival.	(1)
11	E	boast	Brag and boast both mean to show off about something.	(1)
12	C	flask	Bottle and flask both mean a container for liquids.	(1)
13	E	shore	Coast and shore both mean the place where the land meets the sea.	(1)
14	D	root	Origin and root both mean the source of something.	(1)
15	C	flare	Beam and flare both mean a flash of light.	(1)
16	C	support	Bear and support both mean to carry the weight of something. (To answer this question, pupils must understand that 'bear' has two meanings, and not be distracted by 'strong' and 'fierce', which are qualities associated with the animal.)	(1)
17	D	tunnel	Shaft and tunnel both mean a passage. (To answer this question, pupils must understand that 'shaft' has two meanings, and not be distracted by 'stick' and 'stem'.)	(1)
18	D	squander	Waste and squander both mean to make poor use of something. (Discard means to throw something away.)	(1)
19	D	gap	Void and gap both mean a space.	(1)
20	C	supply	Furnish and supply both mean to provide someone with something.	(1)

For more on answering questions involving synonyms, see page 26.

Part 2: Spot the difference

1	D	small	All the other words are colours. (Small refers to size.)	(1)
2	B	quiet	All the other words mean to move quickly. (Quiet refers to sound.)	(1)
3	D	cube	All the other words are two-dimensional shapes. (A cube is a three-dimensional shape.)	(1)
4	C	steal	All the others are types of metal. (Steal means to take something that does not belong to you. Note that this word can be easily confused with the metal steel.)	(1)
5	B	width	All the other words mean very big. (Width refers specifically to how wide something is.)	(1)
6	B	won	All the others are numbers. (Won is the past tense of win and should not be confused with the homophone one.)	(1)
7	C	hour	All the other words mean very small. (Hour is a measure of time.)	(1)
8	D	mast	All the other words are types old floating craft. (A mast is part of a ship.)	(1)
9	A	line	All the other words mean a loud noise. (A line is a straight mark or rule.)	(1)
10	B	disc	All the others are three-dimensional shapes. (A disc is flat.)	(1)
11	C	steam	All the other words mean to over-heat or scorch something. (Steam is the result of boiling water.)	(1)
12	B	opening	All the other words mean to examine something. (An opening is a space in something.)	(1)
13	C	foot	All of the other words mean a phase in a process. (A foot is a part of the body.)	(1)
14	B	ream	All of the other words mean a page in a book. (A ream is a large quantity of paper [500 sheets].)	(1)

For more on answering questions that require you to spot the difference, see page 28.

Part 3: Match the meaning

1	B	fly	is a verb meaning to travel through the air and a noun meaning a type of flying insect.	(1)
2	B	spring	is a verb meaning to bound in the air and a noun meaning the first season of the year.	(1)
3	C	race	is a verb meaning to move very quickly and a noun meaning an event in which people compete.	(1)
4	A	cap	is a noun meaning a cork or bottle seal and a noun meaning something you wear on your head.	(1)
5	D	train	is a verb meaning to work out to improve fitness and a noun meaning a mode of transport.	(1)
6	B	stick	is a verb meaning to fix two things together with glue and a noun meaning a part of a tree.	(1)
7	B	bowl	is a noun meaning a type of crockery and a verb meaning to roll or toss a ball.	(1)
8	D	stalk	is a noun meaning the part of a plant that joins a flower or leaf to the plant and a verb meaning to pursue or track something or someone.	(1)
9	D	change	is a verb meaning to amend something and a noun meaning loose currency.	(1)
10	C	cart	is a verb meaning to pick up and move something and a noun meaning a wooden wheeled vehicle.	(1)
11	B	lead	is a verb meaning to steer a group and a noun meaning a type of metal. Note that the word 'lead' is pronounced differently depending on the meaning.	(1)
12	D	drill	is a verb meaning to penetrate a hole in something and a noun meaning a procedure.	(1)
13	C	figure	is a noun meaning the form of a person or thing and a noun meaning a symbol.	(1)
14	B	term	is a noun meaning a word or expression for something and a noun meaning a period of time.	(1)

For more on answering questions that require you to match the meaning, see page 32.

Part 4: Cloze procedure: choose a word to fit a space

1	D	collected	We collected conkers from under the tree.	(1)
2	B	while	We ate popcorn while we watched the film.	(1)
3	D	healthy	Carrot sticks make a healthy snack.	(1)
4	D	slowly	They walked too slowly so they missed the train.	(1)
5	B	wait	I cannot wait for my party next week.	(1)
6	B	chose	The children chose what they wanted to eat.	(1)
7	E	talented	The actors in the play were very talented.	(1)
8	B	easily	Fragile things are easily broken.	(1)
9	D	forecast	Heavy downpours are forecast for this afternoon.	(1)
10	C	route	Mum carefully planned our route to the seaside.	(1)
11	D	before	You must look both ways before crossing the road.	(1)
12	E	prepare	The girls trained hard to prepare for the race.	(1)
13	B	site	New homes were built on the site of the old car park.	(1)
14	E	lucky	I was lucky to win a prize in the raffle.	(1)
15	A	unexpected	Mia loves books with unexpected endings.	(1)
16	C	conserves	The museum conserves many artefacts from Ancient Egypt. ('Manages' is not the correct answer because although a museum will manage the condition or display of an artefact, it will not manage the artefact itself.)	(1)
17	B	penalties	In medieval times, the penalties for stealing were severe.	(1)
18	D	tranquility	A clap of thunder shattered the tranquility of the forest glade. ('Seclusion' is not the correct answer because it refers to the isolated location rather than its quietness.)	(1)
19	B	bewildered	I was bewildered by the huge choice on the dessert menu. ('Disturbed' is not the correct answer because, although it is grammatically correct, it associates a negative feeling with a choice of desserts, which is usually seen as a positive thing.)	(1)
20	E	evacuated	Everyone hastily evacuated the building when the alarm sounded. ('Abandoned' is not the correct answer because it suggests the building is simply no longer used, rather than being left temporarily in an emergency.)	(1)

For more on answering questions that require you to choose a word to fit a space, see page 34.

CEM 11+ Verbal Reasoning & Cloze Procedure Practice Papers published by Galore Park

PAPER 2

Part 1: Cloze procedure: complete the sentence

1	shone	The Sun shone all day yesterday.	(1)
2	caught	Max caught a cold last week.	(1)
3 & 4	school, theatre	Our school trip to the theatre was brilliant.	(1)
5	station	We arrived at the station just as our train came into view.	(1)
6	salad	They ate salad with their pizza.	(1)
7 & 8	borrowed, library	Tia borrowed two books from the library.	(1)
9	Exercise	Exercise is important as part of a healthy lifestyle.	(1)
10	dramatic	The thunderstorm last night was very dramatic.	(1)
11	difficult	The homework task was not difficult.	(1)
12	Passports	Our passports were checked at the airport.	(1)
13	emigrated	My cousins emigrated to Spain.	(1)
14	barbecue	Mum cooked our burgers on the barbecue.	(1)
15 & 16	Castle, damaged	Windsor Castle was badly damaged by fire in 1992.	(1)
17	league	Our school football team won the league last year.	(1)
18	dangerous	Swimming in the sea can be dangerous.	(1)
19 & 20	villages, traditions	Many villages in England have interesting traditions.	(1)
21 & 22	alpaca, originated	The alpaca is an animal that originated in South America.	(1)
23	campsite	The campsite we stayed at was well equipped.	(1)
24	stationery	I need to get some stationery for the new term.	(1)

For more on questions that require you to complete the sentence, see page 36.

Part 2: Antonyms

1	B	vanish	'appear' means to come into view; 'vanish' means to disappear from view.	(1)
2	D	tiny	'huge' means very big; 'tiny' means very small.	(1)
3	D	rapid	'slow' means to move in an unhurried way; 'rapid' means to move quickly.	(1)
4	D	catch	'throw' means to toss a ball; 'catch' means to grab a ball from the air.	(1)
5	C	narrow	'wide' means broad; 'narrow' means thin.	(1)
6	D	dismantle	'assemble' means to put parts of something together; 'dismantle' means to take apart.	(1)
7	D	brake	'accelerate' means to increase speed; 'brake' means to slow down.	(1)
8	C	danger	'safety' means freedom from risk; 'danger' means peril.	(1)
9	B	unite	'divide' means to split something into parts; 'unite' means to join together. ('Whole' is not the correct answer as it is an adjective rather than a verb.)	(1)
10	D	decline	'accept' means to agree to something; 'decline' means to refuse something. ('Deny' is not the correct answer because it means to say something is not true rather than to turn something down.)	(1)
11	C	absolve	'accuse' means to blame someone for something; 'absolve' means to clear someone of blame. ('Free' is not the right answer because it means to release someone, and this might not necessarily be because they have been cleared of blame.)	(1)
12	D	forget	'recollect' means to remember; 'forget' means to fail to remember.	(1)
13	C	resist	'submit' means to give in; 'resist' means to oppose something. ('Argue' is not correct because one can resist without putting forward an argument.)	(1)
14	D	evaporate	'condense' means to turn into a liquid from a gas; 'evaporate' means to vaporise.	(1)

For more on answering questions involving antonyms, see page 26.

Part 3: Spot the difference

1	C	toe	All the others are parts of the hand. (A toe is part of the foot.)	(1)
2	C	Africa	All the others are countries. (Africa is a continent.)	(1)
3	D	pea	All the others are fruits. (A pea is a vegetable.)	(1)
4	B	acorn	All the others are types of tree. (Acorns are the fruit of the oak tree.)	(1)
5	C	winter	All the others are types of weather. (Winter is a season.)	(1)
6	B	join	All the others mean to cut into something. (Join means to put things together.)	(1)
7	D	chest	All the others are furniture you sit on. (A chest is used to store things in.)	(1)
8	C	spanner	All the others are things that join two materials together. (Spanners are used to tighten or loosen nuts.)	(1)

9	C	action	All the others mean the method in which you do something or plan to do something. (Action is the process of doing something.)	(1)
10	B	route	All the others are highways you travel along, e.g. by car, by foot, etc. (A route is the way you take to get from a starting point to a destination.)	(1)
11	A	disperse	All the other words mean to make something smaller. (Disperse means to spread things out.)	(1)
12	B	small	All the other words mean firm or rigid. (Small refers to size.)	(1)
13	B	stall	All the other words mean to imprison something. (Stall means to delay something.)	(1)
14	D	fury	All the other words mean to provoke someone. (Fury means anger.)	(1)
15	A	store	All the other words mean a large group of individuals. (Store means to keep something safe.)	(1)
16	B	permit	All the other words mean to have earned a reward. (Permit means to allow.)	(1)
17	A	understand	All the other words mean to accomplish your potential. (Understand means to comprehend something.)	(1)
18	D	living	All the other words mean to people a place. (Living means to occupy a place.)	(1)
19	B	allow	All the other words mean to agree to something. (Allow means to permit something.)	(1)
20	B	charge	All the other words mean the pace at which something moves. (Charge means to move quickly towards something.)	(1)

For more on answering questions that require you to spot the difference, see page 28.

Part 4: Order the sentence

1	B	whether	We are planning a trip to Cardiff.	(1)
2	B	some	You need to tidy your messy bedroom.	(1)
3	D	shoots	I love growing plants from seed.	(1)
4	A	will	My friends are meeting me at the cinema.	(1)
5	D	them	It is exciting getting letters in the post.	(1)
6	B	well	My cousins can be rather conceited.	(1)
7	B	the	I was tired by the time the match ended.	(1)
8	D	us	We collected shells from the beach to take home.	(1)
9	E	be	Their donation will benefit all of the children in the community.	(1)
10	B	being	The answer to the question was obvious when I thought about it.	(1)
11	A	this	I mistakenly took the wrong turning by the station.	(1)
12	A	home	The loyal dog followed its two owners wherever they went.	(1)

For more on answering questions that require you to order the sentence, see page 40.

CEM 11+ Verbal Reasoning & Cloze Procedure Practice Papers published by Galore Park

PAPER 3

Part 1: Synonyms and antonyms

1	A, M	select, pick	select and pick are similar in meaning to 'choose'.	(1)
2	E, G	dirty, filthy	dirty and filthy are opposite in meaning to 'clean'.	(1)
3	B, I	entire, complete	entire and complete are similar in meaning to 'whole'.	(1)
4	C, O	final, last	final and last are opposite in meaning to 'first'.	(1)
5	K, N	create, devise	create and devise are similar in meaning to 'invent'.	(1)
6	D, L	finest, top	finest and top are opposite in meaning to 'worst'.	(1)
7	B, H	slumber, nap	slumber and nap are similar in meaning to 'sleep'.	(1)
8	C, K	tardy, late	tardy and late are opposite in meaning to 'early'.	(1)
9	A, M	sudden, unexpected	sudden and unexpected are similar in meaning to 'abrupt', e.g. an abrupt ending.	(1)
10	F, I	dull, blunt	dull and blunt are opposite in meaning to 'sharp'.	(1)
11	E, G	quake, tremble	quake and tremble are similar in meaning to 'shake'.	(1)
12	D, O	damp, moist	damp and moist are opposite in meaning to 'dry'.	(1)
13	H, K	bestow, present	bestow and present are similar in meaning to 'give'.	(1)
14	A, E	squat, low	squat and low are opposite in meaning to 'high'.	(1)
15	B, N	track, tail	track and tail are similar in meaning to 'follow'.	(1)
16	C, L	bygone, past	bygone and past are opposite in meaning to 'present'.	(1)
17	F, J	tale, story	tale and story are similar in meaning to 'narrative'.	(1)
18	G, O	wile, cunning	wile and cunning are opposite in meaning to 'sincerity'. ('Flawed' is not the correct answer because it means imperfect but not necessarily insincere.)	(1)
19	D, F	glee, delight	glee and delight are similar in meaning to 'triumph'.	(1)
20	C, N	abandon, reject	abandon and reject are nearly opposite in meaning to 'embrace'.	(1)
21	G, O	winnings, haul	winnings and haul are similar in meaning to 'jackpot'.	(1)
22	A, E	flimsy, slight	flimsy and slight are opposite in meaning to 'sturdy'.	(1)
23	K, M	predict, foretell	predict and foretell are similar in meaning to 'divine'.	(1)
24	B, J	circumspect, steady	circumspect and steady are opposite in meaning to 'rash'.	(1)

For more on answering questions involving synonyms and antonyms, see page 26.

Part 2: Cloze procedure: choose a word to fit a space

1	C	rescued	The lifeboat rescued the crew of the boat.	(1)
2	B	because	We all laughed because the joke was funny.	(1)
3	E	long	It took a long time to find a parking space.	(1)
4	A	lined	The class lined up in the playground.	(1)
5	C	saving	I am saving up for a new bike.	(1)
6	E	with	Alice loves to go bowling with her friends.	(1)
7	C	crowded	In the summer, airports become extremely crowded.	(1)
8	D	obscured	Our view of the sea was obscured by trees.	(1)
9	C	precariously	The squirrel dangled precariously from the branch.	(1)
10	B	warily	We made our way warily over the fragile ice.	(1)
11	C	exhausted	Ben was exhausted by the end of the race.	(1)
12	B	sharpened	Our cat sharpened its claws on the post.	(1)
13	A	carefully	The fragile vase was carefully packaged for the journey.	(1)
14	C	plates	Volcanoes often form where plates on the Earth's surface meet. ('Pieces' is not the correct answer because the correct term for sections of the Earth's crust is 'plates'.)	(1)
15	B	devastated	In 1666, the Great Fire of London devastated the capital of England. ('Battered' is not the correct answer because this type of damage is associated with storms rather than fire. Pupils should use their historical knowledge of the fire to eliminate 'relocated' and 'skirted'.)	(1)
16	D	usually	There are usually twenty-eight days in February. (Every leap year [every four years] there are 29 days in February. It, therefore, cannot be 'sporadically', which means occurring at irregular intervals. 'Only' does make sense because the other months of the year contain 30 or more days; however, 'usually' is the best fit because there are not always twenty-eight days.)	(1)
17	D	habitat	Loss of habitat is one of the main reasons a species becomes extinct.	(1)
18	C	unanimous	With all jurors in agreement, the verdict was unanimous.	(1)
19	B	scarce	For animals living in desert regions, sources of food can be scarce. ('Absent' is not the correct answer because animals would not be able to live in deserts at all if there was no food.)	(1)
20	C	Inclement	Inclement weather dogged the hikers.	(1)

For more on answering questions that require you to choose a word to fit a space, see page 34.

Part 3: Order the sentence

1	A	some	There were seven puppies in the litter.	(1)
2	D	them	I took a coat in case it got cold.	(1)
3	A	will	Our class had a special assembly today.	(1)
4	E	was	We are going to France this summer.	(1)
5	B	such	The rain eased and the Sun burst through.	(1)
6	C	it	I bought a postcard to send to a friend.	(1)
7	B	all	The paths through the forest all looked the same.	(1)
8	C	to	It will be too wet to play if it continues to rain.	(1)
9	B	on	Following the map, we took the third turning on the left.	(1)
10	D	flake	The snow fell, covering the garden in an icy blanket.	(1)
11	B	more	Realising we were late, we walked faster.	(1)
12	B	my	I went to bed early, although I was too excited to sleep.	(1)

For more on answering questions that require you to order the sentence, see page 40.

Part 4: Match the meaning

1	D	rock	'rock' is a verb that means to move slowly back and forth; it is also a noun that means the hard substance the Earth is made of.	(1)
2	B	space	'space' is a noun that means the area outside the Earth's atmosphere; it is also a noun that means an area that is empty.	(1)
3	C	rose	'rose' is an adjective or noun that means a reddish-pink colour; it is also a noun that means a type of flower.	(1)
4	B	lie	'lie' is a verb that means to say something that is not true; it is also a verb that means to be in a horizontal position, rather than standing or sitting.	(1)
5	D	park	'park' is a noun that means the area of grass and trees around a large country house; it is also a verb that means to drive a vehicle into a space where it can be left.	(1)
6	A	band	'band' is a noun that means a flat, narrow strip; it is also a group of people.	(1)
7	B	strain	'strain' is a verb that means to sieve or filter something; it is also a noun that means pressure or stress.	(1)
8	D	fine	'fine' is an adjective that means to be in good health; it is also a noun that means money that must be paid as a punishment.	(1)
9	B	flag	'flag' is a verb that means to signal something to stop, e.g. a car; it is also a noun that means a piece of cloth on a pole used as a symbol for something, e.g. a country.	(1)
10	D	fawn	'fawn' is a verb that means to flatter someone who is powerful; it is also a pale brownish colour.	(1)
11	C	wake	'wake' is a noun meaning the track left in the water behind a boat; it is also a verb meaning to become awake again after sleeping.	(1)
12	B	liberal	'liberal' is an adjective that means to give a lot of something; it is also an adjective that means to be open-minded about things.	(1)
13	A	buckle	'buckle' is a noun meaning a fastening, e.g. the buckle on a belt; it is also a verb meaning to bend or give way under pressure.	(1)
14	E	concentrate	'concentrate' is a verb meaning to consider closely; it is also a verb meaning to strengthen.	(1)

For more on answering questions that require you to match the meaning, see page 32.

CEM 11+ Verbal Reasoning & Cloze Procedure Practice Papers published by Galore Park

PAPER 4

Part 1: Find the missing letters

1	flav<u>ou</u>red	ple<u>as</u>ant	(1)
2	dis<u>tur</u>b	vi<u>sio</u>n	(1)
3	ver<u>ti</u>cal	trou<u>bl</u>e	(1)
4	phy<u>si</u>cal	pin<u>eap</u>ple	(1)
5	au<u>tum</u>n	flo<u>uri</u>sh	(1)
6	ori<u>en</u>tal	la<u>sag</u>ne	(1)
7	pl<u>as</u>tic	cla<u>ssi</u>c	(1)
8	comm<u>un</u>ity	cur<u>tai</u>n	(1)
9	env<u>elo</u>pe	pur<u>po</u>se	(1)
10	len<u>ie</u>nt	spa<u>rro</u>w	(1)
11	cir<u>cu</u>it	re<u>ve</u>nge	(1)
12	fli<u>ck</u>er	cele<u>bri</u>ty	(1)
13	dun<u>geo</u>n	war<u>rio</u>r	(1)
14	bis<u>cui</u>t	eter<u>na</u>l	(1)
15	pin<u>na</u>cle	for<u>tun</u>e	(1)
16	re<u>mor</u>se	ph<u>anto</u>m	(1)
17	la<u>ure</u>l	len<u>ti</u>l	(1)
18	res<u>po</u>nse	or<u>chi</u>d	(1)

For more on answering questions that require you to find the missing letters, see page 20.

Part 2: Cloze procedure: complete the sentence

1	act	The f<u>act</u>ory manufactures cars.	(1)
2	ice	We could hear the vo<u>ice</u>s of the children next door.	(1)
3	tee	A s<u>tee</u>p path led up the hill.	(1)
4	kin	I love ba<u>kin</u>g in our new kitchen.	(1)
5	awe	I hunted in the dr<u>awe</u>r for the missing sock.	(1)
6	fen	Bella de<u>fen</u>ded the goal brilliantly.	(1)
7	ion	Sailing is his pass<u>ion</u>.	(1)
8	mar	He looked s<u>mar</u>t in his new clothes.	(1)
9	eel	I am f<u>eel</u>ing much better today.	(1)
10	ark	The diamond ring sp<u>ark</u>led in the sunlight.	(1)
11	ail	Jade f<u>ail</u>ed her exam.	(1)
12	tab	We took the pony back to the s<u>tab</u>le.	(1)
13	one	It is important to be h<u>one</u>st.	(1)
14	err	We sat on the t<u>err</u>ace.	(1)
15	yes	The ugly building was a real e<u>yes</u>ore.	(1)
16	ore	Sam ad<u>ore</u>s chocolate cake.	(1)
17	and	The stream me<u>and</u>ers through the valley.	(1)
18	arc	The grass was p<u>arc</u>hed by the heat.	(1)
19	asp	W<u>asp</u>s flew everywhere.	(1)
20	use	My family has just bought a new ho<u>use</u>.	(1)

For more on answering questions that require you to complete the sentence, see page 36.

Part 3: Antonyms

1	brave	An antonym for timid is brave. The 'ra' completes the word correctly.	(1)
2	beneath	An antonym for above is beneath. The 'nea' completes the word correctly.	(1)
3	flexible	An antonym for rigid is flexible. The 'lexi' completes the word correctly.	(1)
4	stingy	An antonym for generous is stingy. The 'ing' completes the word correctly.	(1)
5	frail	An antonym for sturdy is frail. The 'ai' completes the word correctly.	(1)
6	famous	An antonym for obscure is famous. The 'mou' completes the word correctly.	(1)
7	spacious	An antonym for cramped is spacious. The 'acio' completes the word correctly.	(1)
8	random	An antonym for systematic is random. The 'ndo' completes the word correctly.	(1)
9	hostile	An antonym for benign is hostile. The 'osti' completes the word correctly.	(1)
10	partial	An antonym for entire is partial. The 'arti' completes the word correctly.	(1)
11	forbid	An antonym for permit is forbid. The 'orbi' completes the word correctly.	(1)

12	flawed	An antonym for perfect is flawed. The 'lawe' completes the word correctly.	(1)
13	hinder	An antonym for assist is hinder. The 'inde' completes the word correctly.	(1)
14	folly	An antonym for wisdom is folly. The 'oll' completes the word correctly.	(1)
15	virtue	An antonym for vice is virtue. The 'rtu' completes the word correctly.	(1)
16	detour	An antonym for route is detour. The 'tou' completes the word correctly.	(1)
17	frugal	An antonym for extravagant is frugal. The 'ruga' completes the word correctly.	(1)
18	delay	An antonym for expedite is delay. The 'ela' completes the word correctly.	(1)
19	flamboyant	An antonym for modest is flamboyant. The 'mb' and 'ya' complete the word correctly.	(1)
20	affirm	An antonym for negate is affirm. The 'fi' and 'm' complete the word correctly.	(1)
21	amateur	An antonym for professional is amateur. The 'ma' and 'eu' complete the word correctly.	(1)
22	apathetic	An antonym for keen is apathetic. The 'pa' and 'het' complete the word correctly.	(1)
23	discord	An antonym for harmony is discord. The 'i' and 'cor' complete the word correctly.	(1)
24	replica	An antonym for authentic is replica. The 'epli' and 'a' complete the word correctly.	(1)
25	forestall	An antonym for facilitate is forestall. The 'ore' and 'a' complete the word correctly.	(1)
26	denounce	An antonym for endorse is denounce. The 'ounc' completes the word correctly.	(1)

For more on answering questions involving antonyms, see page 26.

Part 4: Cloze procedure: choose a word to fit a space

1	delivered	Some beautiful flowers were delivered to the house.	(1)
2	new	Our new teacher has lots of good ideas.	(1)
3	prey	Owls catch their prey in their sharp talons.	(1)
4	nutritious	A carefully planned diet includes lots of nutritious food.	(1)
5	impressive	Our hotel had an impressive view of the sea.	(1)
6	confided	Sally confided in me and made me promise to keep her secret.	(1)
7	essential	It is essential that all homework is completed.	(1)
8	centenary	The centenary celebrations marked the town's one hundredth anniversary.	(1)
9	opaque	I could not see clearly through the opaque glass.	(1)
10	exploited	Rich Victorian factory owners often exploited children, making them do dangerous work for very little money. ('Paid' is not the correct answer because, while the sentence makes it clear the children were paid, the fact that they were paid little and worked in a dangerous environment means they were exploited.)	(1)
11	hemispheres	The equator separates the northern and southern hemispheres. ('Poles' is not the correct answer, because while the equator is between the poles, they are separated by thousands of miles of land.)	(1)
12	evaded	Legendary outlaw Robin Hood evaded capture, robbing the rich to give to the poor.	(1)
13	exclusively	Native to China, panda bears feed exclusively on bamboo.	(1)
14	environmental	Reducing plastic waste has become an environmental priority.	(1)

For more on answering questions that require you to choose a word to fit a space, see page 34.